Yoga
For
Beginners

Monique Joiner Siedlak

OSHUN
PUBLICATIONS

Printed in the United States of America

Second Edition 2018

ISBN-13: 978-1-948834-64-3

Publisher
www.oshunpublications.com

Disclaimer
All the material contained in this book is provided for educational and informational purposes only. No responsibility can be taken for any results or outcomes resulting from the use of this material. While every attempt has been made to provide information that is both accurate and effective, the author does not assume any responsibility for the accuracy or use/misuse of this information.

Notice

This book is not intended as a substitute for the medical advice of physicians. The reader should regularly consult a physician or therapist in matters relating to his/her health and particularly with respect to any symptoms that may require diagnosis or medical attention.

Yoga Poses Photos

Pixabay.com

Freepik.com

Dreamstime.com

Cover Design by Monique Joiner Siedlak

Cover Image by Pixabay.com

Logo Design by Monique Joiner Siedlak

Logo Image by Pixabay.com

Sign up to email list: www.mojosiedlak.com

Other Books in the Series

Yoga for Stress

Yoga for Back Pain

Yoga for Weight Loss

Yoga for Flexibility

Yoga for Advanced Beginners

Yoga for Fitness

Yoga for Runners

Yoga for Energy

Yoga for Your Sex Life

Yoga: To Beat Depression and Anxiety

Yoga for Menstruation

Table of Contents

Introduction to This Book

A huge deterrent to getting into fitness and the routine of it is that it seems like a pretty daunting task. It seems like you need a lot of previous knowledge for a lot of it before you get into. What diet balances you should have, what equipment you need, what sort of work out you need to do, do you want to build muscle, lose fat? You might need to consult a few other people, maybe even join a gym. Why I would put myself through so much, I'm just happy being myself, you think as you spend another day at home.

Yoga for Fitness

The great thing about Yoga is that it can be done anywhere, anytime with very little equipment, usually just baggy clothes (you already have that covered!) and a non-slip mat to begin.

Other than that you just need patience and an open mind. You can't go into yoga without even a little determination. With the right attitude, you'll start seeing results right away.

Starting Yoga by Yourself

ii/ MONIQUE JOINER SIEDLAK

If you want to see how yoga for yourself without having to go out to a class for it (which is recommended because a yoga class is a great atmosphere to build a calm mindset) you can always try YouTube tutorials or a DVD to get started. DVDs or YouTube videos are pretty tailored so they'll suit your needs. Plus YouTube is always free so if you actually get into it, you'll have more motivation to go back.

Mountain Pose (Tadasana)

The Mountain Pose can be employed as a resting pose or a preliminary pose for just about any standing asana. Even though this pose appears easy, it is great for improving your posture and body alignment, toning the spinal nerves, and creating a sense of consciousness throughout the body. As a pose in itself it's useful to practice. Simply stay in the pose for thirty seconds to one minute, breathing easily.

How to Do

Stand with the sides of your big toes coming into contact with each other. Your heels somewhat apart so that your second toes are matching. Elevate and expand your toes and the balls of your feet afterwards lay them gently down on the floor. Rock back and forth and side to side. Bit by bit decrease this move to and fro to a standstill, with your weight steadied equally on your feet.

Secure your thigh muscles and raise the kneecaps, without strengthening your lower belly. Raise the inside ankles to build up the inside arches. Begin to visualize a line of energy all the way up along your inner thighs to your groins, and from there through the core of your torso, neck, and head, and out through the top of your head. Turn the upper thighs somewhat inward. Elongate your tailbone in the direction of the floor and raise the pubis to the navel.

Pressing your shoulder blades into your back, broaden them crossways and drop them down towards your back. Without moving forward your lower front ribs, raise the top of your sternum straight toward the ceiling. Extend your collarbones, hanging your arms alongside your torso.

Square the top of your head straight over the middle of your pelvis, with the bottom of your chin parallel to the floor, throat soft, and the tongue wide and flat on the floor of your mouth. Soften your eyes.

Benefits

Improves posture, strengthens abdomen and buttocks. Can relieve back pain and decreases flat feet.

Tip

Use a block in the middle of the thighs. The block should be rotated so that the short end looks towards the front. With your legs, squeeze the block and roll it somewhat backward to feel the meeting and turning of the thighs. Take a number of breaths this way.

Then remove the block but replicate the action of your thighs as is the block was there. You don't have to use the block every time, but it helps to remember what rolling it back felt like.

Downward Facing Dog Pose (Adho Mukha Svanasana)

Downward Facing Dog Pose is one of the traditional Sun Salutation sequences poses. It's also an excellent yoga asana all on its own.

How to Do

Begin with your hands and knees in a tabletop position. Make sure your shoulders are aligned above your wrists and your hips are aligned above your knees. Come to a flat back by lengthening the spine. Place your head and neck in a non-aligned position, staring down in the direction of the floor.

Breathe out and raise your knees away from the floor. At the start, keep your knees slightly bent and your heels lifted away from the floor. Lengthen your tailbone positioned from the back of your pelvis and press it slightly toward the pubis. Alongside this tension, raise the resting bones in the direction of the ceiling, and from your inner ankles pull the inner legs up into the groin.

Followed by letting your breath out, push your top thighs back and extend your heels against or down toward the floor. Making sure that you do not lock them, straighten your knees and steady your outer thighs, rolling the upper thighs inward slightly, narrowing the front of the pelvis.

Firming the outer arms, press the bottoms of your index fingers assertively into the floor. From these two points, lift alongside the inside of your arms from the wrists to the tops of the shoulders. Firm your shoulder blades against your back then widen them and draw them toward the tailbone. Keep your head between your upper arms; not allowing it to simply hang.

Continue in this pose somewhere between one to three minutes. Afterward, bend your knees to the floor with a breath and repose in the Child's Pose.

Benefits

Downward Facing Dog pose can help decrease back pain through strengthening the whole back and shoulder girdle. It aids in stronger hands, wrists, the Achilles tendon, low-back, hamstrings, and calves, as well as increasing the full-body circulation. Elongates your shoulders and shoulder blade area. Decrease in tension and headaches by elongating the cervical spine and neck and relaxing the head. It can also lessen anxiety and expand your respiration

Tip

You can alleviate the burden on your wrists by employing a block beneath your palms or you can be capable of completing the pose upon your elbows. By lifting your hands on blocks or the seat of a chair, you can help to release and open your shoulders.

Upward Facing Dog Pose (Urdhva Mukha Svanasana)

Upward Facing Dog Pose is one of the most commonly known, as well as Downward Dog Pose, and recognized yoga pose due to its many benefits and healing uses. Similar to the Cobra Pose, it is thought of as one of the simplest of the back-bending poses and is implemented during the traditional Sun Salutation sequence.

How to Do

Lie face down on the floor. Stretch your legs back, with the tops of your feet on the floor. Bend your elbows and stretch your palms on the floor at the side of your waist so that your forearms are somewhat elect to the floor.

Breathe in and press your inner hands firmly into the floor and somewhat back, similar to trying to push yourself forward along the floor. Then at the same time, straighten your arms and lift your torso up and your legs a few inches off the floor on an intake breath. Keep the thighs firm and somewhat turned inward, the arms firm and turned out so the elbow creases face forward.

Press your tailbone toward your pubis and lift pubis toward your navel. Contract the hip positions. Stiffen but do not totally harden the buttocks.

Steady your shoulder blades against the back and puff the side ribs forward. Lift through the top of the sternum but make an effort not to push the front ribs forward. It will prompt the lower back to tighten. You will at that point look forward or you can angle your head towards the back slightly, remembering to take care not to constrict the back of your neck and the tightening of your throat.

Even though Upward Facing Dog Pose is one position used in the traditional Sun Salutation sequence, you can correspondingly practice this pose independently, maintaining the pose fifteen to thirty seconds, inhaling slowly. Release back to the floor or lift into the Downward Facing Dog pose along with an exhalation.

Benefits

Upward Facing Dog helps open the chest and strengthens the whole body and aligns the spine and invigorates nervous system and the kidneys.

Tip

Performing Upward Facing Dog will elongate and strengthen your whole body. You can use it as a backbend by itself, or as a transition for even deeper backbends.

Cat Pose (Marjariasana)

The Cat Pose consists of relaxation of your back by taking on a posture of a cat. It is generally used to begin a yoga exercise, following the initial establishment of breath, by going through cat and cow pose. Amidst a nice steady foundation in tabletop, this movement allows us grounding as we begin to gently open up the back body and stimulate the core. It's most indispensable goal, though, is the opportunity it enables to combine the breath with activity.

How to Do

Start off by placing yourself in a tabletop position, using your hands and knees as the four legs of a table. Your knees would be positioned up and down below your hips. Your shoulders, wrists, and elbows should be parallel and perpendicular to the ground. You will then focus your eyes on the floor, with your head in a middle position.

Let your breath out and allow your spine to curve by directing it upward to the ceiling. Your shoulders and knees should be in the recommended four-legged position. At this moment, let your head somewhat fall towards the floor. Do not fall so far that your chin is pressed into the sternal hollow of your chest.

While inhaling, once again come back to the typical tabletop position. Maintain breathing in and breathing out deeply while transferring your position from relaxed to alert. Maintain until you feel the relaxation in your spine.

Benefits

The Cat Pose gradually works your spine as well as its muscles. It stretches your neck, back, and torso. In addition to improving the functions of your belly organs, it calms your mind by alleviating it from tension and stress.

Tip

The Cat Pose is an easy and simple yoga pose to relax your fatigued body. Ask your partner or friend to lay a hand in the middle of your shoulder blades if you are finding it challenging to bring a curve in the upper section of your back which will then result in a prompt triggering of that area.

Cow Pose (Bitilasana)

The Cow Pose is regularly instructed in sequence with the Cat Pose to do a mild warm-up sequence. When practiced together, the poses help to stretch the body and prepare it for other activity.

You will inhale through the Cow Pose and exhale through the Cat Pose.

How to Do

Begin with your hands and knees in a tabletop position. You should make sure you align your shoulders above your wrists and your hips are aligned above your knees. Come to a horizontal back by lengthening the spine. Place your head and neck in a non-aligned position, staring down in the direction of the floor.

Breathe in and curve your back. Elevate through your glutes and the crown of your head and allow your belly to drop toward the floor. Rotate the shoulders up and down the back, feeling the back bend in your thoracic spine. Widen up your chest.

Hold the Cow Pose for one breath. Exhale and come back to a nonaligned, tabletop position again. You can also practice this in combination with the Cat Pose, alternating inhales with the Cow Pose and exhales with the Cat Pose.

Benefits

This is a gentle backbend that works with the Cat Pose to awaken the spine. Opens the chest, shoulders and upper back. Teaches the connection between inhaling and expanding and exhaling and contracting.

Tip

Care for your neck by widening your shoulder blades and pulling your shoulders down, away from your ears.

Three Legged Downward Dog Pose (Tri Pada Adho Mukha Svanasana)

The Downward-Facing Dog is one of the best well-known poses in yoga. This adaptation, with one right raised high, urges your balance while opening your hips.

How to Do

Starting in the Downward Facing Dog, breathe in; raising your left leg off the floor behind you. Maintain your hips even with one another as you raise the left leg. Your hips would remain aligned with the floor. Keeping an equally distributed amount of pressure in both of your arms, continue to release the right heel in the direction of the floor.

Lengthen through the raised left heel and the top of your head. Subsequent to holding the pose with the hips aligned for several inhalations, you can open the left hip, stacking it over the right hip. This will permit the left leg to extend higher and provide you with a proper hip stretch. Although you are opening the hips, work to keep the torso from turning to the left. In the open hips position, you can tilt the right knee and allow the right heel to come toward your left buttock.

After several breaths, straighten the right leg and re-square your hips toward the floor. Release the right foot back to the floor. Take several breaths in Downward Dog followed by repeating the sequence on the left side.

Benefits

Three-Legged Downward Dog pose builds up your arms and core. Help improves your hips agility and increases the consciousness of your hip posture.

Tip

Be sure that you do not point the right heel while you lift the left leg. Maintain the heel stretching in the direction of the floor. Don't be concerned about just how high your left leg stretches. It is more essential to maintain the hips aligned in the beginning.

Tree Pose (Vrksasana)

Tree Pose is a yoga pose that will aid you in increasing your stability and mental focus. It could also help you build up the muscles in your legs and core. The lower body offers the assistance for the upper body in this pose.

How to Do

Following the Mountain Pose, bend your left knee transferring all the weight into your right leg. Afterward, direct the left knee to the left wall placing the heel at the side of the right leg.

Look towards the floor and focus at one point. Gradually move as high up as you can maintain your balance, your left foot up the right leg. Once you are balanced at this point, slowly bring the palms together, in a prayer posture in front of your heart.

Keep on focusing at your focal point on the floor. Keeping your right leg forcefully pressing your foot into the floor, maintain your left knee bent ninety degrees towards the side wall. Your shoulders should be down with your back and the chest is pushing forward.

If you are extremely balanced at this point, take a crack at the next phase by breathing in and raising your arms over your head. The arms begin in the football field goal position. You can place your palms together with the thumbs intersected, or your fingers can be intertwined with the index finger pointed up. The fingers are reaching up and the shoulders are down and back.

Breathe and hold for five to ten breaths. To release, slowly exhale the arms down and then release the legs back into the Mountain Pose. Repeat this pose on the other side.

Benefits

The Tree Pose increases balance, memory, concentration, and focus, as well as strengthening the ankles and knees. The Tree Pose extends the groin, torso thighs, and shoulders. It tones your abdominal muscles and develops strength in your calves. This pose also helps to improve flat feet and is beneficial for back trouble.

Tip

First off, take your time. Carefully go through the directions for the Mountain Pose before performing the Tree Pose. It offers the physical basis for this pose.

Stabilize your weight completely throughout your standing foot Attain the position in your hips, tailbone, pelvis, and abdomen; followed by in your collarbones, shoulder blades, arms, and neck. Lengthen the pose through the top of your head. Once you are prepared, you can then lift your arms in the air.

At no time should you lay the foot of your elevated leg completely on your knee or on the side of your knee joint.

Even though the consistent practice of the Tree Pose will tone up the abdominal muscles, your weaker abdominal muscles can cause it challenging to balance.

Chair Pose (Utkatasana)

The Chair Pose is a standing yoga posture that tones your entire body. The Chair Pose is an important component of Sun Salutations and is also often used as a transitional pose. It can also be practiced on its own to help build strength and stamina through your entire body.

How to Do

Begin with the Mountain Pose. Your big toes should be in contact of each other and your heels should be fixed a little apart. Your lower belly has to be drawn in a little to help support your spine. Move your shoulder blades downward keep your chest open and pushed out across your shoulders.

Take a deep breath and raise your arms over your head. You can keep your arms parallel to each other or just keep them up with the palms joined, facing inward. Your arms should be held at the same height or in front of your ears.

Bring your lower ribs toward your pelvis. At that point, breathe out and bend your knees. Try to make your thighs as parallel to the floor as you can. Your knees should come out in front of your feet. The torso should lean a little forward over the thighs till the torso makes a right angle with the upper part of the thighs. Your inner thighs should be parallel to each other and they should push the tops of your thigh bones to the heels.

Keep the edges of your shoulders firm. Bring your tailbone downward to the ground and towards your pubic bone to extend your lower back.

Remain in this pose for thirty seconds to one minute. To release, straighten your knees while you breathe in. Afterward, breathe out and bring your arms to the sides of your body, back into the Mountain Pose.

Benefits

The Chair pose exercises the spine, hips and chest muscles. It also helps to strengthen the lower back, torso and toning the thigh, ankle, leg and knee muscles.

Tip

Practice this near a wall to help you remain in the pose. You can stand with your back near the wall just a few inches away from it. Keep a proper distance to when you come into position, your tailbone comes into contact it then supported by the wall.

Bridge Pose (Setu Bandha Sarvangasana)

The Bridge Pose is a beginning backbend that helps to open your chest and stretch your thighs.

How to Do

To begin, lie supine (on your back). Fold your knees and keep your feet hip distance apart on the floor, ten to twelve inches from your pelvis, with your knees and ankles in a straight line. With your arms beside your body, place your palms faced down.

Breathe in, while slowly lifting your lower back, middle back and upper back off the floor. Gently roll in your shoulders. Touch your chest to your chin without bringing the chin down. Support your weight with your shoulders, arms, and feet. Feel your buttocks firm up in this pose. Both your thighs should be parallel to each other and to the floor.

You could interlock your fingers and push your hands on the floor to lift your torso a bit more up if you want or you could support your back with your palms. Keep breathing easily.

Hold this pose for a minute or two and then exhale as you gently release the pose.

Benefits

The Bridge Pose strengthens your back, opens the chest, and improves your spinal mobility.

Tip

After you roll your shoulders under, be sure not to pull them away from your ears. This often overstrains your neck. Raise the tops of your shoulders toward your ears and push your inner shoulder blades away from your spine.

Triangle Pose (Utthita Trikonasana)

The Triangle Pose is a standing yoga pose that tones the legs, improves stability and diminishes stress.

How to Do

Start in the Mountain Pose. On an exhaling, step your right foot backward about three to four feet putting it parallel to the backside of your mat.

Angle your right foot in somewhat roughly fifteen to degrees, and line up the heel of your right foot with the heel of your left foot. Applying straight legs, firm your thighs without gripping into your knees, and bore the edge of your right big toe into your mat to begin and lift the arch of your front foot.

With an inhalation, spread your arms to shoulder height beside your body, parallel to the floor. Grasp out actively through the fingertips of both hands, palms facing down, and soften the tops of your shoulders.

Enter by extending your right hand forward and pivot at your right hip to bring your right hand down, having your front body and pelvis facing toward the left edge of your mat. Place your right hand on a block just outside the pinky toe edge of your right foot, if you have one. Place your right hand lightly on your right shin for support if a block isn't available.

Stretch your left arm straight up in the direction of the ceiling, firming your shoulder blades onto your back and widening the length from your middle fingertip on one arm to middle fingertip on the other arm when both arms are held out straight at your sides.

Lengthen evenly through both sides of your torso, and press into the support under your right hand to grow taller through your left fingertips and broaden across your collarbones.

Root down evenly through the four corners of both feet, paying particular attention to the outer edge of your back foot, which has a tendency to collapse inwards.

Keep your head in a neutral position or send your gaze up toward your left hand if it feels comfortable for your neck.

Stay in the pose for three to five full breaths. On an inhalation, send your look down and press firmly into the soles of both feet to bring yourself back vertical to stand, and step forward to the top of your mat. Reverse your feet and repeat on the other side.

Benefits

Opens your chest, shoulders and strengthens your legs, extends your groin, hamstrings, and hips.

Tip

If you feel unbalanced in the pose, support the back of your torso or your back heel against a wall.

One Legged King Pigeon Pose (Eka Pada Rajakapotasana)

The One-Legged King Pigeon Pose typically known as the Pigeon Pose is a strong hip-opener that can help increase your flexibility and the scope of motion in your hip joints.

How to Do

Start off in Downward-Facing Dog pose, or on your hands and knees in the Table Pose. Bringing your left knee in the middle of your hands, place your left ankle close your right wrist. Lengthen your right leg behind you so that your kneecap and the top of your foot and toes lie on the floor.

Pushing with your fingertips, raise your upper body away from your thigh. Elongate the front of your body, while releasing your tailbone back toward your heels. Work on aligning your hips and the front side of your torso to the front of your mat.

Drawing down through your front-leg shin, balance out your weight equally in the middle of your right and left hips.

Flexing the front of your foot, press down through the tops of all five of your toes and the back of your foot, as you set your focus towards the floor.

Hold this pose for up to one minute. To release the pose, gather your back toes, raise your back knee off the mat, and then push yourself back into the Downward-Facing Dog. Repeat this pose for the equal amount of time on the other side.

Benefits

The One-Legged King Pigeon Pose stretches the thighs, groins, and abdomen. It can regularly be felt intensely in particular upper-leg and hip muscles. It eases tension in your chest and shoulders, as it additionally promotes the abdominal organs, which benefits your digestion management.

Tip

For added support, you may place a thickly folded towel or blanket beneath your hip.

Standing Wide Legged Forward Fold Pose (Prasarita Padottanasana)

The Standing Wide Legged Forward Fold is a relaxing forward bend that stretches your hamstrings and back. This pose is from time to time also called the Wide-Legged Forward Bend the Standing Straddle, and, the Straddle Fold.

How to Do

Move your feet apart into a wide straddle. Your feet should be somewhat turned in so that the outside of your feet remain parallel. Start to develop into a forward bend, making sure that your effort is begun by the rotation of your pelvis forward. What you do not do all your forward bending with your spine. Keep a flat back as you move forward. Bringing your hands completely below your shoulders at first, start to walk your hands back, getting your wrists aligned with your ankles, if at all possible. Bend your elbows as you would with the Four-Limbed Staff Pose. You can furthermore make an effort by taking each of your big toes in a yogi toe lock with the parallel hand. You can pull slightly on your toes to increase your forward bend. A different option is to walk your hands back behind your ankles at the same time as you keep your arms straight. Try bringing your body weight onward into the balls of your feet to keep your hips in the same plane as your ankles. Engage your quadriceps and draw them upwards. Remain here for five to ten breaths, lengthening your spine on your inhalations and deepening your forward bend on your exhalations. To come out of the pose, bring your hands onto your hips and hold your back straight as you move up to stand.

Benefits

The Standing Wide Legged Forward Fold stretches your groin, hamstrings, and hips while decompressing your spine. Settles down the mind, reduces fatigue, mild depression, and apprehension.

Tip

If your head can with no trouble touch the floor, try narrowing your posture for a deeper hamstring stretch. If your head is on the floor, you may perhaps want to rise into a tripod headstand. Use blocks beneath your hands if they don't touch to the floor.

Standing Half Forward Fold Pose (Ardha Uttanasana)

The Standing Half Forward Fold stretches and invigorates your spine and legs. An essential part of the Sun Salutations This pose helps to prepare your body for deeper yoga poses. It is often known as the Half Forward Bend or the Half Standing Forward Fold.

How to Do

Begin in the Mountain Pose. Lay your hands upon your hips, exhaling, and bend forward from your hips instead of your waist. Pull your abdomen slightly in and concentrate on lengthening your upper body as you go deeper. With your knees straight, set your fingertips or palms on the floor alongside your feet, or hold the rear of your ankles with your palms. Overlap your forearms and maintain your elbows to adopt this pose. Make an effort to elongate your upper body a fraction more on each inhale. On each exhale, release fully into the bend. Remain in this posture for thirty seconds to one minute. To come out of this pose, bring your hands back to your hips and pivot at the hip joints until you are standing tall. Note: do not basically roll your spine up. To aid in toning your thighs, force your heels into the floor as you lift your sitting bones upward the sky, and twist the tops of your thighs somewhat inward. Allow your head to hang loose as it releases all tension from your back and shoulder blades.

Benefits

The Half Standing Forward stretches and elongates your hamstrings, calves, and front as well as strengthening your back and spine, boosting your posture. Practicing this pose stimulates the abdominal organs and belly, improving digestion.

Tip

As part of the Sun Salutation sequence, this pose additionally helps to show the combining of breath with a movement which soothes and calms the mind.

Garland Pose (Malasana)

The Garland Pose is a hip-opening yoga posture that aids in lengthening and opening the hips. An excellent pose to ground yourself.

How to Do

Begin by squatting with your feet as close together as possible, keeping your heels on the floor if you can; otherwise, support them on a folded mat.)

Separate your thighs somewhat wider than your torso. While exhaling, lean your torso forward and fit it between your thighs.

Pressing your elbows against your inner knees, move your palms to together in the Salutation Seal, by pressing your palms and fingers and together. To expand, push your inner thighs against the edges of your torso. Bring your arms forward. Next swing them out to the sides and spot your shins into your armpits. Pressing your fingertips to the floor, or reaching around the outside of your ankles, hold onto your back heels.

Hold this position for thirty seconds to one minute. Next, inhale, straighten your knees, and stand back into the Standing Half Forward.

Benefits

The Garland Pose works at stretching your ankles, groins and back torso and tones the belly

Tip

If you find squatting is difficult, try sitting on the front edge of a chair, with your thighs forming a right angle to your torso. Keep your heels on the floor ahead of your knees. And lean your torso forward between the thighs.

Plank Pose (Kumbhakasana)

As part of the Sun Salutation sequence, the Plank Pose is an arm balancing yoga pose that aids in tightening up your abdominal muscles and strengthening your arms and spine.

How to Do

This pose very similar to as if you were about to undertake a push-up. After completing the Downward Facing Dog, bring your hips forward till your shoulders are over your wrists and your entire body is in one straight line from the top of your head to your heels.

Be sure that your hips don't drop toward the floor or elevated up in the direction of the ceiling. Spreading out your fingers, push them down and balance on your palms. Bend your elbows and remember not to lock them.

Push back through your heels. Shift your shoulders away from your ears. Keeping your neck aligned with your spine, look towards the floor.

Benefits

The Plank Pose tones all the core muscles of the body, including the abdomen, chest, and low back. It strengthens the arms, wrists, and shoulders, and is often used to prepare the body for more challenging arm balances. Plank also strengthens the muscles surrounding the spine which improves posture.

Tip

When practicing the Plank Pose for several minutes, it will help builds endurance and stamina, while toning the nervous system.

Cobra Pose (Bhujangasana)

The Cobra Pose is a familiar Yoga backbend. When you perform the Cobra Pose, you stretch the front of your torso and spine.

How to Do

Lie face down on the floor. Extend your legs back, with the tops of your feet on the floor. Stretch your hands on the floor beneath your shoulders. Squeeze the elbows back into your body. Push the tops of your feet, thighs, and pubis powerfully into the floor.

On an inhalation, start to straighten your arms to raise your chest off the floor. Go only to a height at which you can sustain a connection throughout your pubis to your legs. Press your tailbone toward the pubis and raise the pubis toward your navel. Narrow the hip, compressing but don't harden your buttocks.

Firm the shoulder blades against the back, puffing the side ribs forward. Lift through the top of the sternum but avoid pushing the front ribs forward, which only hardens the lower back. Distribute the backbend evenly throughout the full spine.

Hold the pose anywhere from fifteen to thirty seconds, breathing freely. Release back to the floor with an exhalation.

Benefits

The Cobra Pose is best known for its capability to build up the flexibility of your spine. It stretches the chest along with strengthening your spine and shoulders. It further assists in opening the lungs and stimulating the abdominal organs, improving digestion.

An energizing backbend, the Cobra Pose can reduce stress and fatigue. It also firms and tones the shoulders, abdomen, and buttocks, and assists in easing back pain.

Tip

The Cobra Pose will be able to energize and warm up the body, getting it ready for the deeper backbends in your yoga routine.

Fish Pose (Matsyasana)

The Fish Pose is performed often as a counterbalance poses to the Shoulder Stand Pose. It stretches your upper body in the opposite way. The Fish Pose has a lot of possibilities because it encourages the throat and crown.

How to Do

Begin by lying on your back. Keeping your feet are together, relax your hands at the side of the body. Inhale. With palms facing down, place the hands underneath your hips. Draw your elbows close to each other and exhale.

Elevate your head and chest, and then inhale. You should extend your legs with your head relaxed back, without adding pressure on your head.

Keeping the chest elevated, lower the head backward and touch the top of your head to the floor. Exhale; allow the chest to open finding awareness of relaxed backbend.

Hold this pose for as long as you can while taking soothing long breaths in and out. With each exhalation, relax in the pose. Raise your head, while lowering your chest and head to the floor. Bring your hands back along the sides of your body and relax.

Benefits

The Fish Pose can help headaches caused by stiffness of the neck. It relaxes Spinal Cord and back muscle tissues. It aids in relieving asthma and respiratory disorders. This yoga pose, when practiced regularly, helps to remedy impotence. Also eases anxiety, mild backache, fatigue and menstrual pain.

Tip

If your head does not comfortably come to the floor, position a blanket or block under your head or slightly lower your chest.

Hero Pose (Virasana)

The Hero Pose is one of the most classical seated yoga postures that stretch the thighs and ankles while improving posture. It is one of the most ancient and traditional postures used for meditation and breathing exercises.

How to Do

Begin in a straight kneeling pose with your hips over your knees and the tops of your feet flat on your mat. Keep your knees together, moving your feet to either side until they are roughly a foot and a half away from each other. You should be extending your feet apart to make space for your bottom to descend to the floor between them, while your feet are separating but the knees are staying together.

Take care that you are not sitting on your feet, but somewhat between them with the tops of your feet on your mat, with your feet pointing straight back, not turning in or out. Lower your shoulders away from your ears, resting your hands in your lap.

Benefits

The Hero Pose strengthens your arches, stretches your thighs, knees, and ankles.

Tip

If at any time you are experiencing pain or extreme discomfort in your knees, raise the sit bones on a block. If you are going through sensation in the tops of the feet or ankles, try tucking a rolled up blanket or a folded towel beneath the feet for added support.

If your knees begin to bend apart, loop a strap around your thighs to keep the legs together and put off overusing the inside muscles of the thighs.

Legs up The Wall Pose (Viparita Karani)

The Legs up the Wall Pose is an upturn pose where you lie on the floor against a wall and position your legs together vertically against the wall.

How to Do

If you are performing the assisted version, place a firm pillow or cushion on the floor against the wall.

Start off the pose by sitting with your right side against the wall. Your lower back should rest against the bolster if you're using one. Slightly turn your body to the right and bring your legs up onto the wall. On the other hand, if you are using a pillow, shift your lower back onto it before bringing your legs up the wall. Use your hands for balance as you transfer your weight.

Drop your back to the floor and lie down. Relax your shoulders and head on the floor. Transfer your weight from side-to-side and move your buttocks close to the wall. Allow your arms to rest open at your sides with your palms facing up. If you're using a pillow, your lower back should at this time be totally held by it.

Allow the part of your bone that connects in the hip socket (the top of your thigh bones) to release and relax, dropping in the direction of the back of your pelvis.

Close your eyes and hold for five to ten minutes, as you breathe with mindfulness.

To release, slowly boost yourself away from the wall and slide your legs down to the left side. Use your hands to help press yourself back up into a seated position.

Benefits

This pose reduces fatigue, cramping in the legs and feet and stretches the back of the legs. It can be an excellent pose for alleviating swollen ankles and calves triggered by long periods of standing pregnancy, and travel. It furthermore elongates the front of the upper body as well as the back of the neck and can be helpful for relieving mild backaches.

Tip

Use your breath to ground the tops of your thighs bones into the wall, which assists in the release of your abdomen, spine, and groins. Imagine in the pose, which each inhalation is falling through your upper body and pushing the tops of your thigh bones closer to the wall. Next with each exhale, hold your thighs to the wall and let your upper body extend over the bolster away from the wall and onto the floor.

Corpse Pose (Shavasana)

The Corpse Pose is typically performed at the end of a yoga sequence. It can on the other hand be utilized at the start to calm your body before performing or in the midpoint of a sequence to rest. When applied at the conclusion of a yoga practice it is usually followed by a seated meditation phase to re-incorporate the body mind spirit back into the world.

How to Do

Lying on your back let your arms and legs drop open. With your arms at about forty five degrees from the side of your body, make sure you are comfortable and warm. With your eyes closed begin with slow deep breaths through the nose.

Allowing your entire body to become soft and heavy, let it relax onto the floor. As your body relaxes, feel your full body expanding and decreasing with each breath. Glance over your body from your toes to the top of your head, inspecting for any tension, stiffness or tightened muscles. Intentionally let go and relax any spots that you may find. Sway or shake those parts of your body from side to side to boost further release.

Let go of all control of your breath, your mind, and your body. Allow your body to move deeper and further into a state of complete relaxation. Remain in the Corpse Pose for five to fifteen minutes.

To release the Corpse Pose gradually deepen your breath, wriggle your fingers and toes, bring your arms over your head and stretch your entire body, breathing out, bend your knees into your chest, then roll over to one side going into the fetal position. Once you are ready, slowly inhaling, rising up into a seated position.

Benefits

The Corpse Pose allows your body and mind the time to sort out what has occurred during a yoga session. To most individuals, no yoga session is finished without this final pose. Your body needs this time to comprehend the new information it has received during the practice of yoga. Even though the Corpse Pose is a resting pose, you are not going to sleep.

Tip

Simply, relax. Follow your breathing without striving to control it. Observe what's taking place in your body. Gather your thoughts as they come along and let them go.

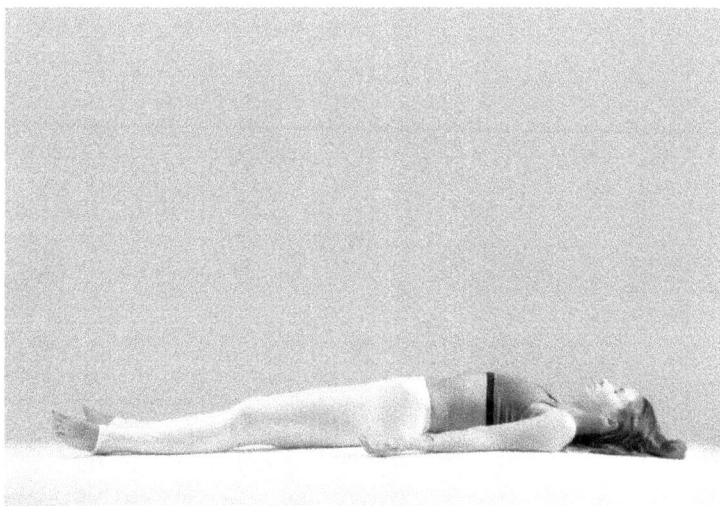

Constructing a Yoga Sequence

Here are a few points to keep in mind how to construct a yoga sequence. You are not at a studio, paying to be there. You do not have to exercise for over an hour. Begin with 5-10 minutes. Notice how you feel by the end of this time. If you feel as if you can do more, go ahead. If no, end your routine there.

Start with 5-10 minutes. By the conclusion of that time, notice how you feel. Do you desire to resume? If yes, continue for an extra five minutes and then check in with yourself once more. If not, close your workout.

The same as any physical journey, a yoga sequence has three clear parts.

Your opening or warm-up sequence

You don't want to jump into the main event tight and cold. This is where you move through and loosening up your major muscle groups as well as body parts

Your main sequence

Once you've warmed up, it's time for your main sequence. This component of your sequence is influenced by the goal of your routine. If it's an asymmetrical pose, keep in mind to do both sides and devote about the same time on each side.

The closing or cool down sequence

Now you've completed the principal portion of your yoga practice, it's time to cool down.

About The Author

Monique Joiner Siedlak is a writer, witch, and warrior on a mission to awaken people to their greatest potential through the power of storytelling infused with mysticism, modern paganism, and new age spirituality. At the young age of 12, she began rigorously studying the fascinating philosophy of Wicca. By the time she was 20, she was self-initiated into the craft, and hasn't looked back ever since. To this day, she has authored over 35 books pertaining to the magick and mysteries of life. Her most recent publication is book one of an Urban Paranormal series entitled "Jaeger Chronicles."

Originally from Long Island, New York, Monique is now a proud inhabitant of Northeast Florida; however, she considers herself to be a citizen of Mother Earth. When she doesn't have a book or pen in hand, she loves exploring new places and learning new things. And being the nature lover that she is, she considers herself to be an avid animal advocate.

To find out more about Monique Joiner Siedlak artistically, spiritually, and personally, feel free to visit her **official website**.

Other Books by Monique Joiner Siedlak

Mojo's Wiccan Series

Wiccan Basics

Candle Magick

Wiccan Spells

Love Spells

Abundance Spells

Hoodoo

Herb Magick

Seven African Powers: The Orishas

Moon Magick

Cooking for the Orishas

Creating Your Own Spells

Body Mind and Soul Series

Creative Visualization

Astral Projection for Beginners

Meditation for Beginners

Reiki for Beginners

Thorne Witch Series

The Phoenix

Beautiful You Series

Creating Your Own Body Butter

Creating Your Own Body Scrub

Creating Your Own Body Spray

Mojo's Self-Improvement Series

Manifesting With the Law of Attraction

Stress Management

Jaeger Chronicles

Glen Cove

Connect With Me!

I really appreciate you reading my book! Please leave a review and let me know your thoughts. Here are the social media locations you can find me at:

Like my Facebook Page: www.facebook.com/mojosiedlak

Follow me on Twitter: www.twitter.com/mojosiedlak

Follow me on Instagram: www.instagram.com/mojosiedlak

Follow me on Bookbub: http://bit.ly/2KEMkqt

Sign up to my Email List at www.mojosiedlak.com and receive a free book!

If you enjoyed this book or found it useful I'd be very grateful if you'd post a short review on at your retailer. Your support really does make a difference and I read all the reviews personally so I can get your feedback and make this as well as the next book even better.

www.ingramcontent.com/pod-product-compliance
Lightning Source LLC
Chambersburg PA
CBHW071622040426
42452CB00009B/1441